AMERICAN GLASS

1. Pitcher of clear glass; hollow stem contains English shilling of 1827; free-blown, probably New England Glass Co. Metropolitan Museum of Art.

AMERICAN
GLASS

BY

VALENTINE VAN TASSEL

Gramercy Publishing Company
New York

CONTENTS

5

I. GLASS—AMERICA'S FIRST INDUSTRY

In 1632 when Captain John Smith made his report on the new colony of Virginia, he said that "glas" was sent "home." What these first made-in-America articles were has not yet been discovered, but the site of the first glasshouse has been uncovered and the location corresponds with the recorded word. There seems no doubt that glass was the first industry to be established in the New World.

Captain Smith brought to his new colony eight European glassblowers in 1608. A glasshouse was built "neare a myle from James Towne," and on the mainland where plenty of fuel could be obtained. It is almost certain that green glass bottles were made there and perhaps some small panes of window glass were tried. Both are typical products of early American glass factories.

About thirteen years later another glasshouse was built, and this time Venetian glassblowers were instructed to make a few beads for barter with the Indians. Virginians were not to see or understand the manufacture of them nor should the beads be "villified" by overabundance. Recent excavations indicate that this second glasshouse had the same location as the first. Fragments and drippings have been dug from the old floor, but there has been no sign of the beads. Some years ago beads were discovered along the James River near the old town, but these may have come from Europe. What happened to the Jamestown factories is not known. There is a story that the Venetians struck against their overseers—which may have been the first labor trouble in America.

The story of Jamestown, Virginia, is typical of all the glass ventures in seventeenth-century Colonial America. There are practically no records concerning these short-lived plants. From contemporary letters and accounts, it is known that some half-dozen or more glasshouses were established during the century. Conjecture as to products has had to be based on our knowledge of seventeenth-century Colonial life, on conditions in the countries from which colonists emigrated, and on these few extant records mentioning glass. An early document from a New England settler advised newcomers to bring panes of glass as the winters were long and cold. This indicates the desire for glass and also its local shortage. Other letters tell of attempts to make both window glass and spirit bottles.

Historians are constantly searching for new records concerning glasshouses and the uses of glass. Excavations at the sites of early glass factories, such as those recently made at Jamestown, add to the data. The study and analysis of the fragments of glass dug up at Jamestown have already changed earlier ideas as to the quantity of glass beads made in those first glasshouses.

This book reflects the recent knowledge obtained and the new interpretations of old rec-

2. *Wine bottle; green; 8 inches high; South Jersey, possibly Wistar; type made in early factories. Metropolitan Museum of Art.*

ords. An attempt has been made to carefully evaluate the known material. For many reasons the history of American glass will forever remain an unfinished story.

In Salem, Massachusetts, a busy shipping center by 1640, some enterprising men built a glasshouse. Although window glass and bottles were probably the principal products, milk bowls and pitchers were very likely made also, as cows had now been brought to the new country. Since glassblowers have always made offhand or special articles for themselves, a few other items must have been produced.

9

There is ample evidence that at least two glass factories were established by the middle of the seventeenth-century in New Amsterdam (New York City) by the Dutch traders who had settled on Manhattan Island. The great colonizer, William Penn, speaks of a glasshouse on the edge of Philadelphia. However, it is probable that a majority of the early colonists never used a piece of glass, even though some glass was imported and a little was made in this country. In any case the desire for it was here.

II. WISTAR AND STIEGEL

When the collecting of American glass first became popular, most of the early ware was desig-
nated Wistar or Stiegel. Even today, after much
research has clarified the situation, it is hard for
people to give up these identifications. Actually,
there are no pieces which can be positively attributed to the glasshouses of either man.

THE WISTARS

From 1739 to 1780, a remarkably long time for
a Colonial business, Caspar Wistar and his son
Richard maintained a successful glasshouse in
the province of West Jersey (later South Jersey),
near Philadelphia. The elder Wistar, a shrewd
businessman, had operated a brass button factory so successfully that he decided to expand
into the glass field. The Colonists were paying a
heavy duty on imported ware. In addition to
other needs for glass, containers were wanted for
rum, which was increasingly easy to get. Everything pointed to glassmaking as a profitable
business.

A large tract of timber was bought and four
expert glassblowers (trained on the Continent),
came with the understanding that Wistar would

3. *Fragment of bottle excavated at site of Wistar's factory in South Jersey; greenish brown soda glass. Such fragments are studied for clues to types and colors of articles. Metropolitan Museum of Art.*

provide for their immediate needs. They were to share in the profits, but instruct no one else in their craft. The period was a difficult one for any American industry. The rebellious colonists did agree among themselves not to buy imported glass. That helped Wistar's factory. In 1752 Caspar died, leaving his brass- and glassworks to his son.

Richard carried on both businesses well enough to survive the depression years of the Revolution. He advertised window glass, various types of bot-

4. Flask of amethyst in Daisy-and-Square *pattern; 4¾ inches high; pattern-molded, characteristic Stiegel-type. Metropolitan Museum of Art.*

tles and chemical ware, but no tableware. As was the custom in all factories, offhand articles must have been made, but excavations have revealed no pieces to indicate that they were commercially manufactured. Unlike his contemporary, Stiegel, Richard Wistar died before his holdings were sold.

HENRY WILLIAM STIEGEL

In August 1750 young Henry William Stiegel,

5. *Purple paneled vase; pattern-molded. Until recently called Stiegel-type. Due to shape of vase and insufficient evidence of attribution, this American type (none found in Europe), is now considered from a New England factory; nineteenth century. Metropolitan Museum of Art.*

with his mother and brother, landed in Philadelphia. Soon afterwards he went to Lancaster County, Pennsylvania, and began working at Elizabeth Furnace, an ironworks. In 1752 the ambitious young man married his employer's only daughter, Elizabeth Huber.

During the following decade leading colonists were encouraging the boycotting of English goods and the establishment of home industries. Stiegel started making glass in his father-in-law's iron-

6. *Stiegel-type drug bottle; 5½ inches high; free-blown blue lead glass with colored enameled decoration; pewter screw collar. Metropolitan Museum of Art.*

works. Like the other early factories, his made bottles and window glass, but Stiegel soon decided to make decanters, drinking glasses, and other items. In the early seventeen-sixties he went to London and Bristol, where he studied the art of glassmaking and hired workers trained in German, Venetian, and English techniques. These men were destined for his new glasshouse in the new town of Manheim.

Besides the glass factory, workmen's houses, and other buildings, Stiegel built a mansion and furnished it lavishly. He began living in such grandiose style that he was soon locally known as the "Baron." His excessive extravagance in his home and business was too much of a strain for the Revolutionary period, when men were buying arms and ammunition instead of glass. After losing everything, he spent some months in debtors' prison. Although there is no grave marked with his name, his story is carried on in glass and in the town he built.

Stiegel's first factory in Manheim probably specialized in bottle and window glass, but included some tableware. His second factory in Manheim was built in 1769 to make flint and other fine tableware in the style of that produced in England and on the Continent. The Stiegel glassblowers, engravers, cutters, and enamelers imitated so well the glassware in vogue in the European countries from which they came that today it cannot be identified as having been made at Manheim. As yet no piece of glass has a mark which would label it as unquestionably Stiegel ware. The term "Stiegel-type" is now correctly used to indicate the kind of glassware made at Manheim.

Stiegel's advertisements, account books, and memorandums show that he manufactured a wide variety of tableware while continuing to make bottles and window glass. His colored glass was pattern-molded (see Glossary); his flint glass engraved and enameled. Although he made such items as salts, creamers, sugar "boxes," bowls, cruets, and candlesticks, it appears that most of his output was in decanters of various sizes, tumblers, mugs, wine glasses, and small containers for medicines, mustard, and smelling salts.

7. *Free-blown wine glasses of Stiegel-type; engraved decoration; 4 inches high. Metropolitan Museum of Art.*

While most of Stiegel's pattern-molded designs (using flutes, ribs, diamonds, and daisies) were imitations of those used abroad, the daisy pattern has not as yet been connected with any foreign factory, and may have been a Manheim design. Daisy patterns (daisy in a diamond or a hexagon and variants), were used mostly on pattern-molded pocket bottles. Some students believe that the *Diamond-above-Flute* is another pattern that originated at Manheim.

In various newspapers from Pennsylvania to Massachusetts, Stiegel advertised his tableware, bottles, and window glass. The later advertisements anounced his "American Flint Glass." (Flint was a term the English used for lead glass.)

8. Engraved Amelung pokal; "New Bremen Glassmanufactory-1788-North America, State of Maryland." Metropolitan Museum of Art.

Following the Continental practice of his day, he used a soda-lime formula for his engraved and enameled ware.

Those who wish to collect the earliest American glass must be content with unauthenticated pieces—articles which may have been made abroad. So-called "Stiegel glass" is continually being sold today. Some of this is definitely Stiegel-type, and some of it has a history that identifies it with Manheim. Some, however, has insufficient background or resemblance to warrant calling it a Stiegel-type. It is advisable for the collector to study the shapes of tumblers, flip glasses, flasks, creamers, bowls, and bottles as well as the various patterns Stiegel is believed to have used for the engraved, enameled, and pattern-molded ware. This can best be done by studying exhibits in up-to-date museums such as the Metropolitan Museum of Art in New York City and by reading books on blown glass such as the recent one by George S. and Helen McKearin called *Two Hundred Years of Blown Glass*. Stiegel-type glass is naturally not plentiful due to the fragileness and age of the ware. It is expensive, but the fun of owning a beautiful piece is commensurate with the very high prices this glass commands.

III. POST-REVOLUTIONARY PERIOD

Glass was in great demand after the Revolution ary War, particularly imported wares. Although the new states soon protected home industries with tariffs on foreign goods, glass manutacturing was usually omitted. Nevertheless, glasshouses were built and at least one, the Boston Crown Glass Company started in 1787, succeeded. Most of the others failed.

AMELUNG GLASS

An interesting attempt was made at "Frederick-Town," Maryland. John Frederick Amelung of Bremen, Germany, built a glasshouse there and for nearly ten years the highly skilled glassblowers he brought from Germany made "all sorts of Glass Ware" from lead and soda-lime formulas. However, neither the loan he obtained from the state legislature nor the inadequate tariff on imported glass in 1789 could keep his business from failing a few years later.

The glass produced there was of outstanding quality. The engraved pieces ranked with the better glass made on the Continent. Fortunately, dated presentation pieces help authenticate other Amelung ware.

9. Light green free-blown ware; c. 1800; probably made at Gallatin's glasshouse, New Geneva, Penna. Carnegie Museum, Pittsburgh.

The collector who has the time and the money to search the area in and around Frederick could make a small collection of this lovely glass. The Metropolitan Museum of New York has several dated Amelung pieces to serve as a basis of comparison. Along with engraved Stiegel-type articles, this early glass might well form the nucleus for an historical collection of engraved ware which could even include the beautiful Steuben glass of today. (President Truman's wedding gift to Princess Elizabeth was a piece of engraved Steuben glass.)

PITTSBURGH GLASS

Although the New Bremen glassworks lasted a very short time, its influence was felt west of the Allegheny Mountains.

In 1797 six of the Amelung craftsmen migrated

10. *Offhand pieces of dark amber bottle glass; "witch" ball covers; early nineteenth century; Pittsburgh area. Carnegie Museum.*

toward Kentucky, but were persuaded to stop at Gallatin's glasshouse at New Geneva on the Monongahela River near Pittsburgh. Albert Gallatin, later treasurer of the United States, started the company but soon sold his share. Christian Kramer, an early shareholder, was an Amelung man. He continued until the middle of the nineteenth-century to practice and to teach apprentices the glassworking techniques he had used at the Maryland glass factory. Kramer and others like him account for the excellent early glass made in the Pittsburgh area.

Almost simultaneously with Gallatin's venture, two former officers in the Revolutionary army—General O'Hara and Major Craig—started a glass business in South Pittsburgh near a coal vein. The proximity of coal and later of natural gas helped develop this area into the great manufacturing district which it became. In the O'Hara-Craig plant, as at the Gallatin-Kramer, window glass and bottles were made along with some tableware.

These early Pittsburgh houses had much the same difficulties encountered by the glassmen along the Coast. There was a scarcity of operatives. The clay for the melting pots were so poor that O'Hara-Craig advertised the huge sum of one hundred dollars to anyone showing them a large deposit of good pot clay. However, they had two important advantages over eastern factories —plenty of fuel and a good market. The cost of transportation over the mountains made the price of imported glass prohibitive. The poorer people bought green bottle glassware and the well-to-do ordered Bakewell's beautiful crystal.

For a long time, collectors paid little attention to glass found in this area. They called the pattern-molded ware a Stiegel product; the good cut ware, imported Irish glass; and the lacy pieces, Sandwich. The pressed and blown Victorian ware was not considered worth while. Glassware in any one of these categories can be found around Pittsburgh and further west. The pattern-molded (called Ohio-Stiegel) and the early cut wares are rarer and more expensive. Later types such as Midwest lacy, *River-boat,* or Wheeling *Peachblow* (see this and later chapters for descriptions of these types), are easier to find, Pittsburgh glass is now coming into its share of appreciation.

BAKEWELL, PEARS AND COMPANY

In 1808, two hundred years after the first glass-

11. Free-blown clear tableware; 1800-1850; typical Pittsburgh shapes, especially galleried rim on sugar bowl. Carnegie Museum.

house was built at Jamestown, Bakewell and Company (later Bakewell, Pears and Company), was established in Pittsburgh. For more than seventy years this company continued in operation and made some of the best American tableware.

Among the first products was cut and engraved table glass which was recognized here and abroad as the equal of imported ware. Bakewell's procured the finest materials and hired skilled English and Irish cutters. When General Lafayette toured the United States in 1825, he visited the factory and was presented with some of its glass which he said was equal to the French. Other early travelers to the Midwest considered the Bakewell factory one of the sights, and often wrote about its "elegant" glass. Deming Jarves, who founded the Boston and Sandwich Glass factory, visited the Pittsburgh glasshouses in 1824 and "paid special attention" to this company. Services were made there for President James Monroe and President Andrew Jackson. Most of the products were sold in the district, which was rapidly increasing in population, or shipped down the Ohio and Mississippi rivers. From New Orleans huge quantities of glass went on to the West Indies, South America, and all over the world.

Besides cut and engraved glass, Bakewell's output consisted of free-blown and molded ware (see Glossary) in both clear and colored. Sometime during its existence the factory tried practically every kind of decoration. As early as 1825, Bakewell recognized the advantage of mechanical pressing and applied for a patent to improve the making of glass knobs. As pressed ware became popular and profitable, Bakewell's made it on a large scale, always following trends in patterns from lacy and simple designs to fancy Victorian ware. Bottles, flasks, and window glass were also manufactured. Indeed, this company was one of the most diversified manufacturers of glass in the early nineteenth century.

THE NEW ENGLAND GLASS COMPANY

By 1819 Bakewell's had its first real competitor for fine glassware in the New England Glass Company at Cambridge, Massachusetts. However, this company was established for the purpose of taking away the New England market from the Anglo-Irish companies. The Cambridge company copied the imported ware so well, that the collector can seldom distinguish the two.

This factory continued making high-grade wares until 1888. Like Bakewell's, its early products were principally fine blown lead glass which was cut and engraved with Anglo-Irish patterns. Lamp fonts, lamp shades, and bottles of various kinds were also made. Some *Blown Three-mold* (see Glossary) was made. Some small objects such as salts were pressed as early as 1820, but pressed glass was never made at Cambridge to the extent it was produced at either the Sandwich factory or in the Midwest. In the period after the Civil War, ornamental glasses such as *Peachblow* and *Amberina* were invented to compete with the Pittsburgh ware. The New England Glass Company was forced to close, like other factories in the area, because competition from Midwestern glasshouses was too great. The latter had better fuel, a better labor supply, and a better market.

LILY-PAD GLASS

While Bakewell's and the New England Glass Company were producing glass in the best European traditions, two American types of ware were developing—first, *Lily-pad* and then *Blown Three-mold*. From the time of Caspar Wistar, South Jersey was an important glass center. After the Revolutionary War the Stanger brothers, former Wistar employees, set up a factory in Glasboro. About 1800 other glasshouses were built in New Jersey, as well as in New York and New England. Most of them made window and bottle glass to supply their own sections.

Whether *Lily-pad* glass was first made by Wis-

12. Lily-pad *aquamarine bowl, light sea-green sugar bowl, and deep dish attributed to New York State factories. Parke-Bernet Galleries, Inc.*

tar workmen is not known. Probably it was started by them and was then made elsewhere as the glassblowers moved on to other factories. Blown out of window or bottle glass, this purely American folk ware did not pretend to imitate or compete with imported articles. The pitchers, sugars, and milk bowls were items that the wives of the glassblowers wanted for use in their own homes. The men followed the old tradition of blowing their own pieces from the tag ends of the melting pots. Whether the superimposed decorations which took the form of a lily pad were added to please their wives or to demonstrate their skill is purely conjecture. When the Jersey workmen migrated to northern factories, they made the same glass at the new locations and passed the Jersey tradition on to their successors so that *Lily-pad* glass was made over a long period, perhaps for a century.

This glassware was blown mostly out of green bottle and window glass; the latter producing the aquamarines which were apparently the most

13. Sugar bowl, jam dish and plate (rare), and tumbler in Blown Three-mold Geometric *patterns, clear glass. Parke-Bernet Galleries, Inc.*

popular. Some amber and a small number of articles in other colors have been found. Also some pieces have glass of a contrasting color added for the decoration. *Lily-pad* ware is rather heavy. Shapes are sturdy yet graceful. The superimposed glass, usually of the same color, was worked up from the bottom into a swag or lily-pad design for the main decoration. Necks or rims were often threaded. Indentations or crimping embellished a handle or foot, and occasionally prunts, seals, and quilling decorated the body. The glass was blown and then worked in a plastic state. *Lily-pad* glass does not appear in the Pittsburgh area, but reached its best form and popularity in the North, especially in New York and New Hampshire.

Collectors can easily recognize this American glass. Its distinctive pattern, weight, color, and obvious handmade appearance set it apart from

14. *Clear glass decanter;* Blown Three-mold Geometric *pattern; pressed wheel stopper. Collection of Mr. and Mrs. Frederick Knight.*

the numerous pressed glass articles found in antique shops. The soft greens and aquamarines are very pleasing to the eye. While this glassware is not plentiful, it can be found in the eastern states. It is suggested as a type for those who wish to have a cabinet collection of definitely American glass.

BLOWN THREE-MOLD

The second American type was a definite attempt to imitate cut glass by a cheaper method. Sometime after the nineteenth century began, glass was blown into molds which had cut glass patterns incised on them. Because the majority of the molds were made in three parts, the glass came to be called *Blown Three-mold* ware.

Since it was difficult in the early 1800's to compete with well-established Anglo-Irish glass-houses, American manufacturers by accident or plan developed this commercial line which proved popular for more than twenty-five years. The variety of items made in *Blown Three-mold* indicates that it was in constant demand. Since glassmen wished their new product to compete with Anglo-Irish ware, they chose similar patterns. Some designs were actually the same as those used simultaneously by the manufacturers of cut glass abroad. Sunbursts popular in cut glass became one of the motifs frequently used in this blown ware. Parallel and intersecting lines adaptable to glass cutting, were used vertically, diagonally, horizontally, and in spirals, with or without the popular sunbursts, daisies, loops, dots, and diamonds. Various combinations of these lines form what is called the *Geometric* patterns, which were produced more extensively than the simpler *Arch* and the more elaborate *Baroque* designs.

The *Arch* patterns are composed of Roman or Gothic arches and may have been used in the early part of the eighteenth century in full-size molds. *Baroque* patterns, which probably came last, are more elaborate and in higher relief. With stars, shells, hearts, palm leaves, and ribbings, the *Baroque* designs approach more closely

15. Decanter in clear Blown Three-mold Baroque
pattern; hollow stopper; 9½ inches high. Metro-
politan Museum of Art.

the popular pressed glass rather than the cut
glass patterns. Designs on the bases are often half
covered by the pontil marks, scars left by pontil
rods. Stoppers vary in design and construction.
Some were blown in full-size molds, others pressed
or pattern-molded. Altogether there are some
one hundred and fifty patterns or variations of
patterns.

Blown Three-mold was produced in many factories from New England to Ohio. A variety of

articles was made in clear and colored glass and some in bottle glass. A few lamp fonts in these patterns were attached to pressed glass bases. *Blown Three-mold* ware can rarely be attributed to any one factory because of its widespread use. It is also probable that moldmakers sold duplicate patterns to different companies.

The molds were usually made in three parts, although two- and four-part molds were also used. In the Irish glasshouses, where some of this glass was made, two-part molds were used. (Unlike cut glass, the patterns of *Blown Three-mold* glass are not sharp. The lines are soft and rounded, often disappearing or running into one another.) After the article was molded, it was reheated for finishing and this further diffused the pattern. ,Mold marks around the tops of articles frequently disappeared altogether. Unlike pressed glass, the pattern on the inside is the reverse of the outside, that is, if the pattern is concave inside, the opposite area outside is convex. An exception occurred when a large gather of glass was used.

The use of the term "three-mold" has been rather unfortunate from the collector's viewpoint. Too often during the last few decades, and even today, collectors and dealers seeing three mold marks on a piece of pressed ware assume that the article belongs to this early nineteenth-century American blown tableware. Mold marks, in themselves, prove just one thing: the article came in contact with a mold sometime during its fabrication. Since even the Romans used molds, there must be other factors in order to attribute the piece to a period or place. Mold

16. Footed bowl; pattern-molded; clear with bluish tone; Ohio-Stiegel. Metropolitan Museum of Art.

marks contribute to the story of an article of glass, but they alone are not sufficient for identification.

For the new or the experienced collector who wishes to collect early American glass, *Blown Three-mold* ware is recommended for several reasons. With a little study the beginner can learn to identify this type of glass. There is an unusually large number of items in the various patterns. There are bottles (decanters, cruets, toilet bottles and castors), tumblers (in varous sizes), pitchers, dishes, bowls (covered or uncovered), saltcellars, celery vases, and other items made in smaller quantities (inkwells, hats, off-hand pieces). Shapes and designs are pleasing, and the collector who finds an amethyst, blue, yellow, or green piece should feel fortunate, as most *Blown Three-mold* was made in clear glass.

17. Cobalt bowl and cruet (center) blown into fifteen-rib mold; right, clear cruet, twenty-four rib mold; Ohio-Stiegel swirled types. Carnegie Museum.

Since *Blown Three-mold* was manufactured in the East and Midwest, it is available to most collectors. Although it is not plentiful or inexpensive, diligent searching will reward the interested person.

Shortly after the beginning of the nineteenth century another technique developed around Pittsburgh and was used for about fifty years. While the Jersey men took their traditions North, Amelung and Stiegel workmen migrated toward the West where they practiced their own techniques of glassworking. The early interest among collectors in Stiegel led to designating this pattern-molded glass made in the Midwest as Ohio-

18. Amber Broken-rib *flask. Metropolitan Museum of Art.*

Stiegel, although undoubtedly it was also made in Pennsylvania and West Virginia.

The shape and pattern of this ware was formed by blowing the gather (see Glossary) into part-size dip or hinged molds. Then it was removed and further continuous blowing expanded the molten metal into the desired size of the flask or dish. The pattern impressed by the mold spread out into a soft delicate outline. While essentially the same technique practiced by Stiegel's men was used in the Midwest, certain features were developed which distinguish it from Stiegel-type pieces. Ribbed, swirled, and diamond patterns

19. Clear sugar bowl and cruet; pillar-molded; River-boat ware; Pittsburgh; amber vase; cobalt bar decanter and creamer. Lowell Inness and the Magazine Antiques.

were the favored designs. The *Broken-rib* was made by dipping the gather into the mold twice. After the gather was blown into a rib mold, it was removed and given a twist. It was then blown into the mold a second time, thus forming the *Broken-rib* pattern. It was removed from the mold and expanded into a flask or dish. The quality and color of Ohio-Stiegel glass are excellent. Forms are pleasing. Flasks, pocket bottles, and flat dishes were the usual items made by this method. This early glass made in the Pittsburgh area is worthy of the attention and interest of the most discriminating collectors of American glass.

20. Free-blown pitcher; South Jersey type; colored looping; type also made in Midwest; c. 1800–1850. Metropolitan Museum of Art.

RIVER-BOAT WARE

A type of glass belonging solely to the Pittsburgh area is the so-called *River-boat* ware. This heavy, pillar-molded glass was sold for river boats, barrooms, hotels, and even for use in homes. The glass was made from a lead formula resulting in clarity and resonance. Although most pieces were of clear metal, there were some colored ones. Because of its weight, *River-boat* glass was sturdy and well adapted to hard use.

21. Light green candlesticks; South Jersey; typical of Post-Revolutionary, free-blown ware, especially gadroon decoration. Metropolitan Museum of Art.

To obtain the thick-pillared design, the gather was cooled slightly and redipped into the pot. It was then blown into a deeply cut mold. This allowed the pattern to appear on the outside while the inside remained smooth. Finally each piece was fire-polished (rotated briefly over flames), to remove any sharp mold marks.

While blown glass continued to be made in the Midwest after the Civil War, it was replaced

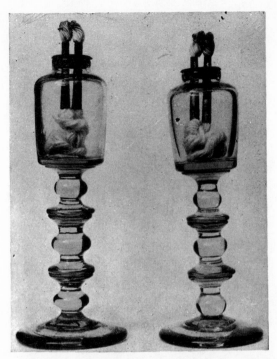

22. *Whale oil lamps; free-blown in clear light green; 9 inches high; early nineteenth century; Metropolitan Museum of Art.*

in most glasshouses by pressed ware. This could be made cheaply enough to be within the reach of everybody.

The collector interested in *River-boat* glass can have fun searching for it in the towns along the Ohio and Mississippi rivers from Pittsburgh to New Orleans. Since it was designed for rougher usage than the thin blown ware, the possessor can feel free to put it to daily use.

23. Lamp with blown-molded top and pressed base; 1825–1850. Metropolitan Museum of Art.

IV. THE PRESSED GLASS ERA

During the War of 1812 to 1814, Anglo-Irish glasshouses stored up a quantity of glass which was dumped on the American market in the years immediately following the peace treaty. This supplied the immediate demands. By 1820, however, industries of the new republic had partially recovered and measures were taken to encourage manufacturers. Legislators were urged to protect the young industries by passing high tariffs. The Franklin Institute was formed in Philadelphia to encourage American production. Emigration went westward and industries expanded in that direction. Glass manufacturers sought cheaper processes to satisfy the ever increasing American demand. *Blown Three-mold* glass was probably the first successful line of American glassware to reach extensive production. It was less expensive than imported cut ware, but still not cheap enough.

Pressed glass was the answer.

In the early nineteenth century both in American and foreign glasshouses a hand press was in use. Pressed feet were attached to such blown articles as bowls and candlesticks. A few small items, such as salts and stoppers, were completely pressed. Deming Jarves himself mentions the im-

41

portation of salts pressed in "metallic molds." Although a hand press was used in Europe, records point to this country as the place where it was mechanized.

Whether an American glassworker, moldmaker, carpenter, or the glasshouse owner himself, whether the inventor was alone or had a partner, just who was the first to mechanically press glass we do not know. As so often happens, experiments with the pressing machine may have been simultaneously successful in several factories. Certainly from 1825 on there was a plethora of patents for the pressing of glass, most of them stating the claim as an "improvement."

DEMING JARVES

Regardless of the inventor, it was Jarves who first saw the possibilities of the glass press. By the time he had obtained his first patent in December, 1828, for an improved glass press, there were a number of companies using the new method. By 1830 so many improvements had been made that mass production of pressed glass was well underway. Pressed glass is characterized by a smooth surface (made by the plunger) opposite the patterned surface (made by the mold).

Deming Jarves was responsible for a great deal of beautiful glass prized by modern collectors. In 1825 he founded the Boston and Sandwich Glass Company on Cape Cod. Although blown and cut ware was made there from the beginning, the idea of pressing articles larger than salts was in Jarves's mind. Other glasshouse owners were also thinking about pressed glass, for patents were

24. *Rosette curtain knobs of pressed glass; opalescent white; c. 1830–1864. Metropolitan Museum of Art.*

taken out in successive years by Bakewell's of Pittsburgh, the New England Glass Company at Cambridge, Massachusetts, as well as the Boston and Sandwich Glass Company. Jarves patented many improvements and his factory produced greater and greater quantities of it, eventually including sets of stemware and tableware, as well as candlesticks, vases, lamps, bowls, and souvenirs, in clear and colored glass.

LACY WARE

As in the case of *Blown Three-mold,* the first pressed glass was made to compete with or imitate cut glass. Early patterns followed closely the typical designs of cut ware, but very soon a new characteristic appeared. This was the fine stippling which covered the backgrounds, resulting in lovely delicate patterns. It was given the name "lacy" and was a style entirely different from anything in cut ware. Whether or not Jarves obtained the idea from the French or vice versa is not known. By the 1830s the glassworker although still important for making free-blown ware, was

43

secondary to the designer and moldmaker in the pressed-glass departments.

The lead formula used for lacy ware gave the intricate patterns, brilliance and the pieces a weight not found in modern reproductions. Many articles, however, show defects in manufacturing. Sometimes the batch was poorly mixed with the result that bits of unfused sand or bubbles of air appear in the glass. Often the unpatterned surface is uneven and rarely is it as smooth to the touch as in blown glass. Irregularities occurred when the temperature of the glass or of the mold was not right, the plunger was out of alignment, or the mold skidded. Since it takes considerable skill for a glassworker to judge the amount of hot metal to drop into a mold, the edges of the early dishes were often of uneven thickness. Among the improvements patented was a ring to prevent the escape of glass along the rim. In piece molds, glass was squeezed out along the seams by the pressure from the mold. It formed fins which were sharp and hairlike instead of rounded as in blown ware. These fins could not be removed from lacy glass without affecting the pattern. Later designs such as *Ashburton* and *Thumbprint* were adaptable to fire-polishing, which was in general use about 1840. Gradually, open and shut molds were improved and eventually the complete article was made in one operation. Nevertheless, throughout the nineteenth century the glass press was manipulated by hand and many articles were made by the combined processes of pressing and blowing.

25. *Eagle cup plate; clear lead glass. Metropolitan Museum of Art.*

CUP PLATES

The first articles to be pressed were those which were easy to make, particularly salts, knobs, and shallow dishes which included the little cup plates. In the early days of the century cups without handles were used for tea. The hot amber liquid was poured into the saucer to cool. To save the linen and the table top, the cup was set on a small china plate. Jarves saw a large market for cup plates of pressed glass. The first plates he made followed rather closely the motifs of cut glass such as fans, strawberry diamonds, and the like. Soon lacy backgrounds were used. About one thousand different cup plates have been catalogued—many of them with but

26. *Historical cup plates: President Harrison, Fort Meigs, Bunker Hill, Henry Clay; c. 1831–1841 probably Boston and Sandwich Glass Co. Metropolitan Museum of Art*

slight variations of design. They have been classified in conventional and historical patterns and offer a fascinating field to the collector.

Conventional designs include the early cut glass patterns, the heart series, the naturalistic, and the geometric patterns.

Historical patterns feature men prominent at the time and events important in the young republic. During the several decades these little plates were made, Henry Clay was an important

American statesman and certainly interested in the welfare of the glass industry. (In 1824 he introduced a tariff to protect American glass manufacturers.) Two plates were made in his honor —*Henry Clay to the Right* (as it is called now), has a lacy background and was probably earlier than *Henry Clay to the Left*. The latter has some ten variations. Other plates commemorated Washington, LaFayette, Harrison, and events, such as the Battle of Bunker Hill or the Hard Cider Campaign. There is not, however, as wide a range of historical subjects in these small plates as in the bottles and flasks of a slightly later period.

Collectors and students of American glass are indebted to Mr. Albert C. Marble of Worcester, Massachusetts, for his excellent classification of these fascinating little articles. Although collecting them has been popular for the last few decades, cup plates are still available, but the colored and historical ones are rather rare. Extensive illustrations and descriptions can be found in various books.

Reproductions have been made of a number of the heart plates, as well as others. (See Ruth Webb Lee's books on reproductions.) The new cup plates are poor imitations in soda-lime glass which has no ring when struck. However, it must be noted that cracked or badly chipped pieces of lead glass will not have a bell-like tone. It is difficult to find perfect cup plates, but small chips out of the scalloped edges are not considered detrimental to the value of a plate. In collecting most glass articles it is better to buy "proof" or perfect pieces. If, however, an article is needed

27. *Pressed sugar bowl; bright blue with milky mottling; color unusual in early pressed ware; Boston and Sandwich Glass Co. Metropolitan Museum of Art.*

28. *Lacy dishes from Midwest; characteristic patterns with coarse stippling. Carnegie Museum.*

29. Candlesticks in popular dolphin shape; clear, greenish yellow, pressed glass; Boston and Sandwich Glass Co. c. 1840. Metropolitan Museum of Art.

to illustrate a type in the collection, a chipped or cracked one is acceptable. Watch for cracks around handles and in pieces that are dusty. Reputable dealers do not sell damaged pieces without informing the customer.

Large plates, saucers, creamers and sugars, covered dishes, bowls, salts, and bases for lamps and candlesticks were made in lacy patterns. Most of them are in clear glass, but some are in colors—transparent, opaque, or opalescent. The charm of lacy ware lies in the brilliant clear glass

49

*30. Thumbprint, an early pattern made in clear
pressed glass sets; Bakewell, Pears and Co., Pittsburgh. Metropolitan Museum of Art.*

where the light is refracted by the multiple edges
or facets of the pattern. The finely stippled backgrounds, which are the main characteristic, in-
crease the sparkle. Some pieces also have a silver
lustre when observed through the top surfaces,
which are always left plain except in the covers
of dishes. The tone of this early glass, which was
made from a lead formula, has the ring of good
cut ware. While the factory at Sandwich produced a large amount of lacy ware, it was also
made in considerable quantities in the Midwest.
There the stippling was sometimes coarser, and

31. Diamond-thumbprint; *pattern used for clear pressed glass table sets. Metropolitan Museum of Art.*

geometric designs using many circles were more popular than at Sandwich.

POPULAR PRESSED PATTERNS

In the late 1830s, times were bad and since lacy ware required expensive molds, it was gradually replaced by simpler patterns. The advent of fire-polishing, which almost entirely eliminated mold marks, may have again encouraged glassmen to attempt imitations of cut glass patterns. The new designs such as *Ashburton, Thumbprint, Diamond-thumbprint* and *Excelsior* were clearly in the cut glass fashion, but they have a charm of their own. About this time, table sets of goblets, plates, pitchers, sugar bowls, compotes, and odd pieces were made so that today's collector can find use for her treasures, if she chooses a pressed glass pattern made in these pieces.

It is difficult to determine in which factories specific patterns were made. In some cases, however, a design has been identified with a definite factory, but that does not guarantee it was not

32. Thousand-eye *pattern in vaseline yellow;
pressed glass. Typical plate with bent corners;
sugar bowl (lower right), a variation without the
three knobs. Metropolitan Museum of Art.*

made in other glasshouses too. The place where
a pattern originated is seldom known. Most of
the popular patterns were copied openly or sur-
reptitiously. Some factories made a slight variation in the basic design, others changed only the
name, which is confusing to modern collectors
and researchers.

Many of the early patterns, such as *Ashburton,
Bellflower,* and *Diamond-thumbprint,* were popular after the Civil War, but new ones were continually brought out. As the nineteenth century
progressed, the elaborateness and ornateness of
shapes and designs increased. Eventually the tre-

33. Loop-and-Dart with Round Ornaments; *clear pressed glass; pitcher with applied handle; pattern patented 1869, Portland Glass Co., Me. Collection of Mr. and Mrs. Frederick Knight.*

mendous output of pressed tableware required hundreds of patterns. Thus today's collector, with either little or much to spend, can find a pattern suited to her collecting urge.

From 1840 on the number of glass factories increased and production increased even more. With the invention of the cheap soda-lime formula after the Civil War, the quality of the glass declined and patterns took on a greater similarity. The press had been desirable at first because it produced cheaper glass, but it was continually improved to make still cheaper and larger quantities. Under such circumstances something invariably suffers—shape or design, quality of material, or workmanship—and always there occurs that loss of individuality which goes with handicrafts. To stimulate sales, manufacturers offered new designs more and more frequently, and these became less and less good. While a machine could

34. Bellflower *pitcher, left; an early ribbed pattern. Pitcher (right)* Tulip *pattern. Both clear pressed glass with applied handles. Metropolitan Museum of Art.*

press out hundreds of pieces to a glassblower's dozens, it could never equal the perfection of the latter's work. There was plenty of glass for the people, but before the end of the nineteenth century quality had lost to quantity.

Pressed glass offers the largest field for the collector. It has been made continuously since about 1820, which gives collectors a wide range of choice as to types (such as table sets of patterned ware, lacy ware, or decorative pieces), colors, quality, and design. There is great difference in price and availability, partly due to the scarcity of the pattern, partly to its current popularity. Don't choose a pattern at random. Consult the books that specialize on pressed wares. Perhaps it would be wise to start on an inexpensive pattern and sell it later if you wish to change.

The prices of the older patterns, such as *Ashburton, Diamond-thumbprint* and *Bellflower,* vary from four dollars to as much as one hundred and fifty dollars per piece. The post-Civil War pressed ware is less expensive. For example, the popular *Red Block* and *Ruby Thumbprint* range in price from four to twenty-five dollars. The patterns that were made in several colors, such as *Daisy and Button,* are priced according to the color. The clear article is the cheapest while the blue is the most expensive. Yellow pieces are a little higher than amber ones. The pressed ware made around 1900 is very plentiful and often comes as low as fifty cents or a dollar per article.

Pressed glass is fun to collect even if it is not always designed well or produced perfectly. Most patterns are fairly plentiful, and enough can be found to make a pretty setting for parties in either clear or brightly colored ware. Because of its availability and price, this glass is excellent for gifts. The thoughtful friend or member of the family can usually find a suitable or long-desired article. Collectors are always glad to have new pieces on a birthday, at Christmas time, or even when convalescing in a hospital!

V. VOGUE FOR PICTORIAL BOTTLES

Collectors and historians can be grateful to the Connecticut businessman who is reported to have thought of decorating bottles with men and scenes from American history. Our republic was new in the 1820s. The effects of a second short war were just passing. The following decades were full of conflict for industry and government. There were lively events to record and many forceful figures to portray.

Bottles were probably the first articles of glass to be made in America. During the first two centuries of our history, they continued to be the chief product of our glasshouses. From the time they were first made in pre-Christian Egypt and Syria, bottles were used for other liquids than alcohol. Since they were needed for serving, storing, and transporting fluids, many sizes and shapes were manufactured. The majority of bottles were made from glass of the cheapest of soda formulas and by the least expensive methods. Local sands were used with no attempt at removing impurities.

A few types such as scent bottles, ranging in size from those for slipping into a glove to those for dresser sets, were treated in the best fashion of the day. Stiegel listed miniature ones for

35. Gemel bottle with quilling and prunts; used for oil and vinegar; South Jersey; 1800–1850. Philadelphia Museum of Art.

smelling salts. Later, cologne and perfume bottles, as well as cruets and some other types, were also specially designed and decorated. But as a rule early bottles were left undecorated.

The first bottles were free-blown. Later they were blown into wooden molds to shape the bodies. For some time two-piece molds were employed to form all of the bottle but the mouth. This was hand-finished with glassblower's tools. Eventually, the whole bottle was blown into a mold. Then in 1899 Michael Owens at Toledo,

57

36. Bitters bottle, left; one of numerous eagle flasks, right. Metropolitan Museum of Art.

Ohio, designed the first automatic machine for making bottles. The evolution of bottles from the squat, flat bottomed, "black glass" type to the tall bottle of today is an interesting phase in the history of glass.

Early nineteenth-century factories always listed a variety of bottles such as "Druggists and Confectioners Show Bottles," "Apothecary Vials," spirits (bottles for wine), "case" or gin bottles, blacking, ink, and snuff bottles, "Cologne Water" bottles, peppersauce, mustard, cayenne, and pickle jars, "Acid Bottles," and bottles for "Patent Medicine, OIAL, Mineral Water, Tincture," liniments, and smelling salts. There were nursing bottles, gemel or twin bottles, saddle bottles, and quantities of flasks. Bottles were round, flat, octagonal, square (for packing), and of odd shapes. These containers were advertised in vari-

37. Hard Cider flask with plow and flag of Harrison's presidential campaign in 1840. Metropolitan Museum of Art.

ous sizes—demijohns, carboys, quarts, pints, "pocket bottles," and "Packing Bottles, assorted sizes."

"DOCTOR" DYOTT BOTTLES

"Doctor" Dyott, an early dispenser of patent medicines in Philadelphia, made use of bottle molds to advertise himself and his products. By the time of the Civil War, patent medicines, tonics, or nostrums were very popular and bitters bottles (as the containers are called), became a staple product in many glass factories. Unknown to many users, the cure-alls contained alcohol, which greatly stimulated the sale of the products. Later, many bitters were sold in odd-shaped bottles. Bitters bottles were made in greater numbers than commemorative flasks, but the latter are more popular with collectors and often bring very high prices.

By the beginning of the nineteenth century almost everybody drank something alcoholic. Not only did all travelers carry flasks, but bottles of liquor could be found in every home. As fruit trees and grape vines became established in the new country, hard cider, brandies, and wines were made. When the rich lands of the Midwest were put into cultivation, the large grain harvests were used to produce whisky and beer. Bottle factories naturally followed distilleries and breweries. Bottles and flasks became staple products and often helped glasshouses to weather depressions. They were exported in large quantities and rum was imported.

PATTERN-MOLDED FLASKS AND PICTORIAL BOTTLES

Pattern-molded pocket flasks, such as those made in Manheim and later in the Midwestern houses, are of particular interest because of their charm and comparative rarity. The colors (amethysts, blues, ambers, and greens), the texture of material, and the workmanship of these early flasks have rarely been excelled in other types of bottles. The so-called Pitkin flask was a swirled or ribbed flask made by the pattern-molded method, but with two gathers of glass. A few bot-

38. Washington flasks from Dyottsville, 1833–1838. Left, General Taylor on front; green. Right, Washington on front, (Captain Bragg on back); brown. Metropolitan Museum of Art.

tles were produced in *Blown Three-mold* designs.

By the 1820s the new pictorial bottles eclipsed all others in popularity. These were blown in full-size hinged molds so as to retain the picture which the mold impressed in low relief on the glass. Bottle glass in shades of amber and green was most frequently used with aquamarine, the favorite. As with articles of pressed pattern glass, bottles and flasks made in the first two or three decades show better design than those made later, when the glass industry was becoming more and more mechanized. They also depict more of the historical events.

Favorite figures were the presidents—George Washington, John Quincy Adams, Andrew Jackson, William Henry Harrison and Zachary Taylor. Other celebrities also were chosen, among

39. *Dark green flask with horse and loaded wagon on rails; inscribed "Success to the Railroads"; from Keene, N. H.; c. 1830. Metropolitan Museum of Art.*

them, Benjamin Franklin, DeWitt Clinton, Henry Clay, and the Marquis de Lafayette. Only the American eagle appears more often than Washington, and on some bottles both are seen, each on a side. Bottles representing later presidents show them in connection with their political struggles, or with election slogans and scenes. Many bottles also have on one side a picture of the glasshouse where they were made.

Manufacturers took advantage of the passing scene. The enterprising Doctor Dyott depicted

Lafayette while the General was touring this country. P. T. Barnum, having paid a tremendous price to bring the Swedish Nightingale to America, got her name and picture on everything from bonnets and pianos to bottles. A dozen or so glasshouses produced special Jenny Lind bottles.

Other bottles have unidentified portraits, symbols of America, historical scenes, and conventional designs. Masonic flasks were made in profusion and there were "slogan" flasks like those marked "Corn for the World." After 1850 designs became stereotyped. The Civil War brought a large number of "Union" bottles, the gold rush had its memorials, and other decorations continued to appear along with events of interest.

As in the case of bitters, bottles began bearing advertisements of the product they contained. In 1860 a distiller, E. G. Booze of Philadelphia, sold his whisky in a log cabin bottle bearing his name, address, the word "whiskey," and the date 1840. Although the word "booze" was used in Elizabethan England, this may have been the origin of its popularity in America.

In this field of bottles the collector can proceed along many lines and in various price ranges. There are a number of extremely rare types and colors, as well as many very common ones. Pictorial bottles or flasks satisfy the collector who desires rare pieces, beautiful colors, handmade, or early American glass. Perfume bottles are favorites, and exquisite pieces from Stiegel-types to the Steuben glass of today can be acquired for an historical collection. Bitter bottles are not as beautiful as many of the other types, but fascinating with their odd shapes and queer advertisements.

This is a field that interests men collectors. There are many who collect glass, including even table settings of pressed ware. Usually older and rarer pieces appeal to men more than later American glass. You can make collecting a family affair with even the children participating. In one family, the father collects pressed glass in wine and cordial glasses, the mother a table setting in pressed ware, and the little boy, glass toys.

VI. THE VICTORIAN ERA IN GLASS

The term "Victorian" does not designate a particular style but rather a period characterized by ornateness, overdecoration, and a kind of stuffiness. The opening up of this country and its industrial expansion in the nineteenth century brought great wealth to some and more money to most of the citizens. It allowed people to fulfill the desire for possessions, to have the same as a neighbor, the rich man, or the celebrity. For most Victorians this resulted in an overabundance of everything. Simplicity gave way to showiness.

In the designing and manufacturing of glass the tendency showed up in several ways. Since every corner of a room, every table and stand had to be filled, a great deal of ornamental ware was produced. As houses were overdecorated, so was much of the glass. Colored ware was pressed in elaborate patterns and also gilded. Cased ware (articles made of two or three layers of contrasting glass), was cut until little was left of the outside layer. A single article was sometimes patterned, ruffled, and appliquéd with flowers. Untrained women enameled thousands of articles with flowers, pastoral scenes, children, and animals.

The size of many articles was in scale with the

40. Satin glass pitcher; soft rose color with white lining; applied wild rose with stems in clear glass; acid treated. Collection of Violet Sherman.

high-ceilinged rooms. Imposing chandeliers, tall lamps, and vases filled the parlors. Large fruit bowls and compotes were necessary for every dining rooms. Victorian ornateness reached its height in tall epergnes—some standing more than two feet high.

Although the developments in glassworking after the Civil War tended toward the production of cheaper ware of poorer quality, some pieces that were made in the late nineteenth century were as beautiful as the earlier articles.

41. Emerald-green blown vase; white enameled figure; typical late Victorian. Author's collection.

While designing for mass production of pressed glass prevailed in most plants, there was also considerable thought and money spent on developing lovely color combinations and decorations in the blown ware. Many collectors prefer it to pieces of early American glass because of the soft coloring and more perfect fabrication.

THE SODA-LIME FORMULA

Pressed ware from about 1870 on changed in both quality of design and in composition. In

1864 William Leighton of Wheeling, West Virginia, formerly from the New England Glass Company of Cambridge, brought out a formula which omitted the expensive ingredient of lead. Glass made from his soda-lime mix did not have the brilliance of the earlier lead ware. It was not as suitable for cutting and engraving, nor even for the simple early pressed glass patterns, which are so attractive in articles of clear lead glass. Nevertheless hundreds of patterns continued to be made in clear glass from Leighton's formula.

The new soda-lime formula, the new improvements in machinery, the new buying power of the public, all produced a boom in the pressed glass business. Clear blown glass with simple cut or engraved designs was still made for an exclusive few. (As yet the machine had not encroached on this craft.) Colored blown glass was developed into the so-called "art glasses" and ornamental ware, some of which achieved ornateness that surpassed the fanciest of the pressed products. Mass production in glass, however, consisted of colored pressed ware with elaborate designs. New patterns were constantly brought out. Those that proved popular were retained longer and manufactured in a greater variety of items. The same patterns were often made in different colors and with variations, usually at different factories. Some of the old patterns like *Ashburton* were produced for a while from the new formula, but the absence of lead spoiled their earlier charm.

Briefly, there are three main types of decoration for pressed ware. First, clear glass was decorated solely by the pattern impressed on it in the mold. The pattern always appears in low

42. *Square, clear pressed sugar bowl;* Rose-in-Snow *pattern; also made round and in colors. Collection of Mrs. Glen W. Giddings.*

relief and the inside of the article is smooth. This type has been used continuously down to the present time. Second, the same technique was used on a transparent or opaque colored glass. Here the appeal lies in both pattern and color. This type includes opaque white ware such as the *Blackberry* pattern. Colored pressed ware was made in quantities after the new soda-lime formula was invented. Third, clear colored or opaque glass has the pattern impressed upon it and is also decorated by other means. The multiple-decorated type belongs to the late Victorian period.

43. Spoon rack in Jumbo *pattern; frosted decoration on clear glass. Metropolitan Museum of Art.*

MULTIPLE-DECORATED GLASS

Soon after the Civil War, acid baths or sprays were used in various ways to decorate both blown and pressed ware. The terms "Camphor," "Satin," and "Frosted" have been applied to this glass, but *Frosted* is more generally accepted. An early and attractive use of acid etching on clear glass is found in patterns such as *Coin and Frosted Leaf* and the more showy *Lion, Westward Ho,* and *Jumbo.*

Extremely popular in the 1890s was a clear patterned glass brushed with a ruby stain. There was also a great deal of enameling done on both

44. Creamer and sugar in Bent Buckle *pattern; clear pressed glass with thin stain of cranberry color on upper half of articles; typical decoration c. 1900. Author's collection.*

opaque and colored transparent glass. Gilt was freely used on edges, on patterns, anywhere to make a piece appear richer. In much of the enameled and gilded Victorian glassware poor workmanship spoiled the decorations.

Opalescent glass was used somewhat during the first half of the nineteenth century. A milky iridescence is found in this earlier ware, but not in later glass made from heat-sensitive opal formulas. The latter usually has an opaque pattern on a transparent background. The popular *Hobnail* glass was first called *Opalescent Dewdrop*. The earliest pieces of it were blown, but later the improved pressing method produced a more even effect. The opacity of the nodules (protruding knobs which give it the name *Hobnail),* is due to the cooling and reheating of the article. *Polka Dot* and *Opaque Fern* were popular types of the later pressed ware. Still another use of the heat-sensitive opal glass was to imitate *Overlay* ware which was cut by hand.

71

45. Tumblers. Left to right, Polka Dot *pattern, blue (heat-sensitive);* Inverted Thumbprint *in* cranberry Spatter; *blown amethyst with golden flecks.* Fern *pattern, white;* Diagonal-ribbing, *blue and white (both heat-sensitive glasses). Author's collection.*

TYPES OF CASED GLASS

Cased glass was not r.ew in the nineteenth century but became very popular. The term "cased" is applied to glass of more than one layer of contrasting colors (with or without a clear layer). These layers can be put together by several different methods, and frequently are referred to as lining, plating, or flashing. Usually the terms "plating" and "flashing" are applied to glass that has a very thin outside layer.

The Romans knew how to make cased glass. The famous Portland Vase in the British Museum in London is the product of their skill in design and glassworking technique. A shell or cup was formed and set in a container while a gather of a contrasting color was quickly and gently blown into it. The two were fused and the article finished according to the decorative effect desired.

72

*46. Amberina punch bowl, cups, and ladle;
blown glass;* Inverted Thumbprint *pattern; New
England Glass Co., c. 1883. Collection of Mr.
and Mrs. George Spreng.*

A quicker method of casing is usually called
"flashing," that is, a gather of one glass is covered with a gather of a contrasting color, and
then finished. By this method a thin layer of one
of the metals could be used, thus saving costly
material such as gold-ruby glass.

During the 1860s cased glass cut in patterns
was popular for vases, lamps, scent bottles, and
a few other items. The outside layer of opaque
white was cut through to form a pattern on the
colored layer beneath. This is generally called

47. *Shaded flashed vase; white lining, deep pink shading to light ruby. Collection of Violet Sherman.*

"Overlay." The designs were simple all-over patterns. The cutting of the pattern required a steady hand and accurate eye. This glass is a favorite of collectors who wish a few decorative pieces.

Cameo glass is a cased ware in which the outer layer forms the design. (The Portland vase is the outstanding example.) The undercoat is the background. A great deal of skill is required to make cameo glass by the old process of hand grinding (on a rotating wheel). The use of hydro-

48. Vase of Burmese *glass; pale yellow shades to pale pink; enameled decorations; leaves fused into vase; white petals and gold dots in low relief. Author's collection.*

fluoric acid in the latter part of the nineteenth century eliminated or reduced to a minimum the handwork.

ART GLASSES OF THE 1880s

By 1880 Midwestern factories were established as the leading producers of glass. Their output in pressed ware for domestic and foreign markets was tremendous. Since factories in the East could

49. Cruet of blown Satin *glass; soft pink to deep rose with covering of clear glass; twisted rope handle ending in flower prunts; acid treated. Collection of Mrs. Harold Emerick.*

not compete in this line, they tried to maintain their business by bringing out more expensive blown wares. These became known as the "art glasses." Like pressed ware, they have their good and bad examples. Few of them proved really profitable.

One of the most popular was the *Amberina* glass, which was produced and patented in 1883 by the New England Glass Company. It was a transparent glass blown in various shapes and patterns, although some pressed and cased pieces were made, though probably not at Cambridge. *Amberina* is one of the many heat-treated glasses.

50. *Collection of* Satin *glass pieces, including a footed bowl (upper) and tall vase (lower right) of* Coralene *glass (beaded patterns). Metropolitan Museum of Art.*

After an article was blown, one end was carefully reheated to produce a lovely ruby tone which blended into the amber of the unheated part. This ruby coloring varies in different pieces from a deep ruby to a cranberry hue. *Amberina* was one of the few art glasses made in a large variety of articles. Collectors can find this lovely glass from Boston to New Orleans.

The opaque shaded glasses such as *Peachblow* (white to pale pink), and *Burmese* (yellow to a soft rose), were made in the same way, that is, one section was reheated to bring out the color. These, however, were usually given a dull mat or finish. *Peachblow* made at Wheeling, West Virginia, had a thin opaque white lining. The

77

51. Cruet of Pomona *glass; pale amber base and neck; flowers slightly bluish; blown hollow stopper. New England Glass Co. Collection of Mrs. Harold Emerick.*

outside layer blended from yellow to deep pink and was left shiny. Like *Amberina,* the *Burmese* glass, which was often decorated with enamels, proved very popular. Queen Victoria, herself, ordered "two pairs of vases."

One of the loveliest of the art glasses is the *Satin* type. It is a flashed glass in combinations of opaque white, clear, and pastel pinks, yellows, greens, and blues. Much of it is shaded. It was molded in herringbone, diamond, and oval patterns, and covered with enough clear glass to fill

52. *Sugar Bowl in* Hobnail *pattern; opalescent pressed glass of ruby red; Wheeling, W. Va.; second half of nineteenth century. Metropolitan Museum of Art.*

the interstices. Usually *Satin* glass was given a dull finish.

Overshot glass was an ingenious attempt at Sandwich to produce something different. The gather was rolled in particles of crushed glass which melted into the surface leaving a rough effect. In *Spangled* ware, flakes of mica sandwiched between layers of colored and clear glass present a bizarre appearance. *Vasa Murrhina* contains bits of colored glass which fused with the original gather to form a variegated ware. Gold and silver flecks were also used. Other at-

79

53. *Basket of amber-threaded Sandwich ware; blown in pattern mold; machine threaded; baskets were popular articles in late Victorian era. Metropolitan Museum of Art.*

tempts such as *Agata, Pomona, Tortoise Shell, Crackled, Threaded, Silvered, Spatter,* and *Lava* glass were invented with the hope of attracting the public's interest.

In contrast to these wares is the beautiful Venetian latticinio and "striped" glass made by Nicholas Lutz at Sandwich. Paperweights with latticinio, millefiori, flowers, fruits, and portraits were ornamental pieces that displayed the skill of the American glassworker. These are collector's items that range in price from twenty-five to several hundred dollars.

Marble glass was an unusual type of pressed ware sometimes called *Mosaic, Slag,* or *End of the Day.* This opaque ware of white with brown, green, or purple resembles marble and was made in considerable quantities. Some collectors scorn this Victorian glass. However, others enjoy the natural patterns which were allowed to form in

54. Striped flask by Nicholas Lutz; white and colored canes. Boston and Sandwich Glass Co., c. 1875. Metropolitan Museum of Art.

the glass when two colors were partially mixed before the blowing or pressing of the article. The purple and white combination is often very attractive.

SOUVENIRS IN GLASS

Glass souvenirs did not first appear at the Philadelphia Centennial in 1876, but much earlier. Little keepsakes or "whimseys" had always been made in blown glass. The cheap pressed

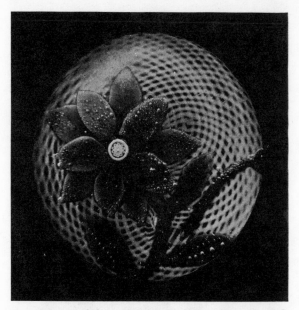

55. *Paperweight; pink poinsettia covered with clear glass; favorite flower at Sandwich factory; dewdrops on petals and latticinio background. From* Old Glass Paperweights *by Evangeline H. Bergstrom.*

glass made them profitable items, especially for fairs and expositions. Plates and tumblers were pressed with pictures of the event where they were to be sold. Small articles such as match and toothpick holders and little creamers and mugs were particularly popular. The mugs were often stained red and engraved with an inscription. Thousands of these small articles were made for the large expositions, such as the Chicago Fair in 1893, as well as the popular county fairs. The juvenile or the adult collector will enjoy these little dated historical articles. Collectors are also

56. Patterned covered bowl. Marble pressed ware often used for table sets. Metropolitan Museum of Art.

57. Goblets and plate of pressed Custard *ware; opaque cream with very light brown touches in a grape pattern.* Antiques Journal.

83

58. Admiral Dewey tumbler of clear glass; Flag-ship, Olympia *on reverse; 1898. Author's collection.*

attracted to the covered animal dishes that were sold in carload lots as mustard containers. One factory advertised them in "barnyard" groups.

After the depression of the early 1890s, a large number of glass factories combined. Many went into the more profitable business of manufacturing lighting ware or containers, the bottles or jars used for storing and packing. A number continued to make cheap pressed glass for the growing premium business as well as for retail trade and for mail-order houses. Some of these glass-

59. Souvenir creamer of pressed glass; Sunk Honeycomb *pattern in clear base; upper part, ruby stain with engraved inscription, (also found without inscription); handle clear. Author's collection.*

houses imitated the patterns in the cut glass popular toward the end of the nineteenth century.

COLLECTING VICTORIAN GLASS

The collector of Victorian glass has a wide choice of styles and colors in either pressed or blown ware. Prices vary considerably from expensive art glasses such as *Amberina,* which actually contains gold, to souvenir mugs that can be purchased for as little as thirty-five to fifty cents. If you have the collecting urge, a visit to several antique shops is advisable. Often some pattern or

*60. Covered animal dishes in opaque white
pressed glass. McKee Bros., Penna. Metropolitan
Museum of Art.*

type will catch your interest. Of course it is wise
to learn as much as possible about the chosen
glass before you undertake serious collecting.

Many collectors start with family heirlooms.
The beginner can often find valuable pieces at
her mother's or grandmother's home. Perhaps the
start of a collection is in a familiar cupboard.
There are also still many unsearched attics.

VII. CUT AND ENGRAVED GLASS

There are many erroneous ideas about cut glass. Some people think of it in terms of the heavy ware made at the beginning of the twentieth century, others as that made in Ireland during the late eighteenth and early nineteenth centuries. Few realize that the art of cutting and engraving glass is almost as old as glass itself. The first cutters were lapidarists who saw in the new material a substitute for precious and semiprecious stones.

The Romans cut shallow geometric patterns on clear glass. By the fourth century A.D. they were cutting pictorial scenes such as chariot races and gladiatorial combats with the names of the participants and of the cutters included.

Rock crystal was cut in considerable quantities in medieval Egypt, Persia, and later in Europe. Since glass resembled it but lacked its clarity, a formula was sought for making glass with the transparency of rock crystal. Although a decolorizing agent, manganese, was used by second-century Romans, it was not until the middle of the sixteenth century that a nearly colorless glass was made by the Venetians. They called it "cristallo." Since then any very clear glass has been called crystal.

In 1676 an Englishman, George Ravenscroft, invented a lead formula which eventually brought about the great popularity of cut glass. The new formula produced glass which surpassed rock crystal and approached the diamond in brilliance of refraction. From that time on, cut glass grew in beauty and popularity. Consequently, in late eighteenth-century America, the most desirable glass tableware was the cut "crystal" from Ireland.

TECHNIQUES AND HISTORY

The difference between cut glass and engraved glass lies in the size of the wheel used for cutting the decoration and in the finishing process. Actually, glass is ground away rather than cut. A rotating cutting wheel (grindstone) is fed with an abrasive and water while the glass is held against it. Stone or metal discs produced what is commonly called cut ware, while small copper wheels produced engraving, which requires the greater skill. Many sizes of copper wheels were used to engrave the finest ware, and this is true today. The cut or engraved surfaces were polished or left unpolished. A combination of techniques was frequently used to afford contrast in the same design. Glass was both shallow and deep cut. The decision was not left to the artist; depth of cutting depended on thickness of glass. Since many articles of early glass had thin walls, shallow cutting was a necessity.

Engraving is shallow grinding. It is used to produce scenes, portraits, and some naturalistic designs. Left unpolished, engraved decoration

61. Salt cellar, free-blown, clear, shallow cutting, New Jersey, c. 1825–1850. Metropolitan Museum of Art.

has a character not attainable by ordinary cutting, which is better adapted to geometric patterns.

Glass in America has been cut and engraved continuously from the times of Stiegel and Amelung. Some of the English and German glassblowers that Stiegel brought to America in 1763 were skilled in this work, and it is probable that much of Stiegel's clear glass was thus decorated. The style of the work and the designs are in the Continental manner, and some of it is rather crude.

At Amelung's glasshouse in Maryland greater skill was used, as is evident in the engraved presentation articles which have been preserved. After the New Bremen Glass Works closed, the

62. *Hanging lantern; clear blown glass; engraved; brass mounts; c. 1800–1825. Metropolitan Museum of Art.*

workers who took the long journey over the mountains to Pittsburgh helped produce there what probably may be considered America's best early glassware.

Those first Pittsburgh glasshouses were started during the Anglo-Irish period (1780–1825) when cut glass was particularly fine. The earlier shallow cutting had given way to a prismatic type in which appeared fluting, slicing, scalloping, circular and oval concavities, and parallel or intersecting grooves, all deeply cut. The diamonds cut in high relief were crisscrossed to make the so-

63. Sugar bowl, clear with greenish tinge; engraved; early Pittsburgh blown glass. Metropolitan Museum of Art.

called strawberry-diamond, so often imitated in later pressed glass. A large quantity of Anglo-Irish cut glass was exported to America.

PITTSBURGH GLASS

While people living along the eastern coast demanded and bought imported ware, those west of the Alleghenies found the crystal cut in Pittsburgh of excellent quality and much less expensive. To transport the English and Irish glass from the cities of the Atlantic coast over the mountains to the Midwest was not profitable. To

64. *Articles of cut glass made by Bakewells; clear lead glass; popular type 1808-1850. Carnegie Museum.*

make glass in the Pittsburgh area, sell it locally, and also send it out along the great Ohio-Mississippi waterway was good business indeed. By 1850 cut ware was made for the palatial river boats, the numerous hotels, and also the private homes along the route.

In 1808 Bakewell's in Pittsburgh were making cut and engraved ware in patterns popular abroad. Many travelers who reached this gateway city lauded in their memoirs or letters the excellence of Bakewell glass. A set was cut for President Monroe in 1817; a medal was won at the Franklin Institute in 1825; an appreciation and favorable comparison with Baccarat's French glass was sent by General Lafayette after his tour in 1825. As other factories were built in the Pittsburgh section, they too cut glass.

The New England Glass Company was prob- ably the first eastern glasshouse to produce a large amount of glass cut and engraved in the Anglo-Irish style. Their product was equal to any other American ware and quite as fine as the imported. At the Boston and Sandwich Company on Cape Cod, Deming Jarves also installed a large cutting shop. Many of the cutters in these early factories had their apprenticeship in Anglo-Irish glasshouses.

By the twentieth century this beautiful cut glass had lost its American identity. Because in patterns and style of cutting it resembled Irish glass, it was for a long time considered to be im- ported. Since the glasshouse at Waterford was better known than its contemporaries in Ireland, quantities of late eighteenth- and early nine- teenth-century cut glass are today miscalled Waterford. (The same kind of error has been made with much of the pressed glass that is cur- rently called Sandwich.) Actually, there were numerous factories producing the same type and quality in both Ireland and America, and very little of it was ever trade-marked.

Besides Bakewell's, the New England Glass Company, and the Boston and Sandwich Glass Company were other factories that made and cut excellent glassware. Among them were the John L. Gilliland Company of New York, Gillerland and Sons (1861–1892) of Pennsylvania, and Dor- flinger's.

Christian Dorflinger built the Greenpoint Glass Works in 1860 at Brooklyn, New York, to

65. *Claret, hock, champagne stemware of cut glass; New England Glass Co., 1880s. Society for the Preservation of New England Antiquities, Boston.*

make fine flint and colored ware. (His first glass-house in Brooklyn was for shades and chimneys for kerosene lamps.) Later he moved to White Mills, Pennsylvania, where he built a third glass-house and continued making excellent quality ware. Dorflinger cut glass for President Lincoln (at the Brooklyn factory), and for Theodore Roosevelt, when he was president. Glass continued to be cut and engraved in the Anglo-Irish manner until the "prismatic" style of cutting came in sometime after the Civil War.

About 1880 deposits of sand almost free from iron were located in the Midwest. This was an important discovery resulting in far finer metal. Cut glass gained a new impetus and even greater popularity. "Those who intend to make birthday, Christmas or wedding presents can not select anything more appropriate and welcome than cut glass," read one advertisement.

In the early factories the cutting shop was often located in a nearby building since the cutting was a separate process and the work was done on "blanks," the cold, finished, but undecorated articles. When cut glass became very popular, uncut blanks were often sold separately to companies who specialized in cutting. (The capital outlay for a cutting establishment was not comparable to that of a glass factory.) Often a skilled cutter would set up a small shop for himself and a few other cutters. Brooklyn and Corning in New York were among the early centers for these shops.

T. G. HAWKES AND COMPANY

In 1880 Thomas G. Hawkes set up a cutting shop in Corning. He bought his fine handmade blanks from the Corning Glass Company. By 1886 the Hawkes Company was making glass for the White House In 1889 two of their cut glass patterns won the Grand Prize in the Paris Exposition. By the end of the nineteenth century the company was known for the best in cut glass. Even after the ware lost its general popularity, the Hawkes factory continued to produce cut glass of finest quality. Since all of their pieces were marked after 1895 (with two hawks), the new collector has easily identifiable glass in the Hawkes ware. A great deal of it has been made for special orders with monograms and even with crests. It offers a fascinating field to the collector who would like an historical collection of the patterns used by various presidents from 1886 to the present, or by well-known American families. Here is a type that has indeed been neglected.

From 1890 to 1910, a period famous for cut

glass, American factories produced a ware that differed appreciably from cut glass of the early 1800s. The glass itself was clearer due to finer ingredients and improved melting processes. Steam-run wheels made deeper cutting easier, although their use was not new to the period.

The thick lead glass, the handmade blanks, and the hours of skilled craftsmanship required for cutting decoration on blanks made this ware expensive. With today's labor prices, the cost of producing tableware of this type would be prohibitive. The collectors who acquire this lovely crystal will have glass that will not be reproduced.

Although early Anglo-Irish glass was deeply cut, the patterns appearing after 1890 were more intricate and often completely covered pitchers, bowls, and candlesticks, even the rims and bases. The upper part of tumblers and necks of bottles were often the only clear areas, and even the latter were sometimes cut. The bases of most pieces had either a continuation of the pattern or a star. Like pressed glass, cut glass was made in sets for tableware. Articles such as chandeliers, candlesticks, candelabra, and vases were popular in early cut ware. By 1900 lamp shades and globes, complete lamps, and dresser sets were also made of cut glass.

"At no previous time have its uses been so many and its varieties so numerous. While the common glass is cheap beyond precedent, the finer glass, made from the best materials and highly wrought by hand, has exquisite beauties to which the world's markets attach high values. It has the luminous brilliancy of colorless cry-

66. *Horseradish bottle; English strawberry-diamond and fan motifs; Dorflinger's. Cruet, cut in
snowflake with plain and notched prism motifs,
Corning, c. 1900. Author's collection.*

67. *Berry bowl; clear lead glass blank pressed
with pattern for cutting; mold marks visible;
inside brilliant silver sheen. Author's collection.*

stal, made by skillful cuttings to sparkle with white light or prismatic colors." Thus one catalogue described its product.

Elaborate cut ware was beyond the reach of the majority, and therefore all the more desirable. Factories making pressed glass soon found a substitute. Instead of selling plain blanks to the cutting shops, they pressed patterns into the blanks. Semiskilled cutters touched them up on the cutting wheel to make them almost perfect imitations of completely handmade articles. The short-cut method allowed a large supply to reach the market and as always happens when a scarce article becomes plentiful, cut glass no longer commanded so high a price. It was just a step to selling pressed blanks without the touching up on the cutter's wheel, and then to making them of cheaper glass. "Near-cut" and "press-cut," as the quantity productions were described, were advertised in mail-order catalogues as perfect imitations of popular cut ware.

By 1895 many factories were making this imitation cut glass. A decade later the deep cutting on hand-blown or machine-pressed blanks was rapidly going out of style. The market was so flooded with cheap imitation cut ware that by the time of World War I only a few cutting shops remained.

Until quite recently collectors of American glass have avoided cut ware because the early cut glass was considered to be Irish ware and the glass cut about 1900 not old enough to be considered an antique. For sometime, however, there has been a market for cut ware in the Southwest. Collecting either table sets (goblets, wines, sherbets, tumblers, plates, and odd pieces) or single decorative pieces, especially large fruit bowls, is becoming more and more popular everywhere. Those who start a collection now will be able to obtain a more complete set faster and more easily, and at a lower price, than in a few years.

The person who likes to collect one class of articles can choose small items such as knife rests, condiment sets, and the inevitable matchholders —hats, slippers, and boots. Cruets and cologne bottles are particularly lovely in cut glass, and powder boxes make very attractive candy containers. A punch bowl with the tray and cups is an expensive but very desirable set.

For the collector who wishes rare or cabinet pieces there are presentation, commemorative, and other special-order articles. Such a one is the large St. Louis punch-bowl set cut for the Libby Exhibit at the World's Fair in 1904.

VIII. THE NEW ART GLASS

The struggle for a new decoration for glass probably began when the art of glassmaking started. In 1907 Edward Dillon, in his book, *Glass,* considered artificial iridescent coatings among the fantastic methods for extrinsically decorating glass. "Perhaps the most elaborate instance of such decoration may be found in the 'favrile' glass of Messrs. Tiffany, the well-known goldsmith of New York."

TIFFANY'S FAVRILE

Louis Comfort Tiffany's interest in the opalescent glass of John LaFarge led him to develop further this new type of glass for church, institutional, and domestic windows. Although he sold many windows, the business did not maintain the glass factory which he had built. He began combining leftover glass with metals for jewelry, hat pins, jewel and snuff boxes. Later he also set vases and lamps of *Favrile* on metal bases.

In 1889 Tiffany saw in Europe an exhibit of old Roman glass which was iridescent from its long burial. Always a lover of the scintillating colors on the backs of beetles and the feathers of birds, he experimented with metallic coatings

68. *"Console set" of* Favrile *glass with green vine motif on the bowl. Iridescent ware designed and signed by L. C. Tiffany. Made at Tiffany Studios, Long Island. c. 1900. Parke-Bernet Galleries, Inc.*

69. *Vases of* Favrile *glass; left, floriform bud vase of gold and peacock blue; 14¾ inches high; right, jar of translucent green with flame red and gold iridescent decoration. Parke-Bernet Galleries, Inc*

70. Vase of Favrile *glass; hooked pattern of iridescent blue; crystal medallions surrounded by engraved sprays. The Brown Jug, Sandwich, Mass.*

for glass and produced the iridescent glass he called *Favrile.* He designed lamps, vases, and bowls of unusual shapes and elaborate patterns, as well as simpler and less expensive tableware. His most famous creation was the *Peacock* design. Skilled glassblowers carried out his ideas. The new ware included a wide range of articles for "drawing rooms, dining rooms and boudoirs." Wall plaques and tiles as well as mosaics were included in the long list of products pro-

71. Vase of opaque Aurene *glass ·with iridescent pattern in red, gold, and green; combination of opaque (body of vase) and metallized (decoration) glass. Author's collection.*

duced at the Tiffany Studios on Long Island.

Tiffany glass was very popular until about 1910. The public found in its irresistible colors a relief from the cut and imitation cut ware then flooding the market. The fact that it was expensive made it all the more appealing, and the name of Tiffany increased its desirability. After Tiffany established a market for his iridescent glassware, inferior imitations were exported to America from Bohemia.

Here in the United States an early competitor of Tiffany was Frederick Carder who came to Corning, New York, in 1903. At Stourbridge in England, he had experimented with metallized glass. After forming the Steuben Glass Works, he made a superior type of metallized glassware called *Aurene*. The classic shapes of Frederick Carder's vases, bowls, and other pieces, the uniform iridescent coating, the artistic naturalistic patterns, and the expert workmanship made much of his work superior to the darker and more ornate Tiffany ware. He also created many lovely designs in *Cameo, Cased,* and *Overlay* glass, in bicolor pieces, and some with applied ornament.

TIFFANY-TYPE GLASS

The Union Glass Works at Sommerville, Massachusetts, attempted the new ware under the name *Kew Blas*. Before the Boston and Sandwich Works closed, experimental pieces were made there but never marketed.

The Quezal Art and Decorating Company of Brooklyn, New York, called their iridescent glass *Quezal,* the name of an American bird that has brilliant feathers of green, crimson, and gold. Victor Durand, a former Tiffany craftsman, who joined the Vineland Glass Works at Vineland, New Jersey, marketed Tiffany-type ware successfully for some years under the name of Durand Art Glass. It was signed either *Durand* or *V. Durand.*

The Harry Northwood Company of Wheeling,

72. Vase of Quezal *glass; green hooked pattern on white ground with iridescent gold spots and four prunt designs. Author's collection.*

West Virginia, from about 1910 to 1920, sprayed pressed glass with metallic oxides to give them an iridescent effect. These were made in various shades of blue and orange, and trademarked with with an *N*. Other companies also made and sold this iridescent ware so cheaply that it was called the "poor man's Tiffany." This glass, which was made particularly in water sets, bowls, and small dishes is now becoming increasingly popular with collectors.

Although *Art Noveau* has not usually been in-

73. Vase of iridescent Durand *glass; engraved leaf sprays. The Brown Jug, Sandwich, Mass.*

cluded in American antique glass, the earliest examples are now between fifty and seventy years old. It is daily gaining wide appreciation among those who love color in glass. As more is known about the skill and technique required in its fabrication, it will be still better appreciated.

When you select a bright blue *Aurene* bowl or a tall slender *Peacock Favrile* vase, give consideration to the surroundings in which it is to be placed. The addition of a matching candy dish or ash tray can make a set which will be a very effective decoration in a living room. Several of the companies discussed made quantities of electric light shades which collectors today are converting into attractive table and boudoir lamps. There are colorful table sets, dresser sets, flower sets of bowl with two candlesticks, and other items to be had in this art glass. Many pieces made by Tiffany, Carder, and Durand will become collector's items. This glass is rather high in price, and little of it is collectible in large sets. It is not only glass to enjoy in your own home, but excellent for gifts to friends who appreciate color and workmanship. Collectors have been slow in realizing the value of this unusual art ware.

IX. GLASSMAKING AND DECORATING

Until the twentieth century there have been few major developments in the art of glassworking. After the introduction of the blowing iron about the first century B.C., there was no comparable invention until the pressing machine in the nineteenth century. In fact, almost every known technique of making or decorating glass up to this machine age was practiced during Roman times. The Venetians rediscovered Roman methods, improved some, and also developed better formulas.

FORMULAS

The basic formula used from the beginning of the art is composed of silica (sand) fused with soda and potash. To this was added lime or lead, as well as oxides for coloring, and manganese or other chemicals for decolorizing. Cullet or broken glass is included in every formula. In spite of manganese, most glass has a greenish tinge which is due to iron in the sand. Another deterrent to good clear glass is the presence of "seeds" or "stones" and "cords" which are caused by unfused sand, foreign matter, or air pockets due to improper melting. In early glass we can often see bits of unfused sand or even dust from the atmosphere.

George Ravenscroft's lead formula, invented in England in the 1670s, produced a great change in glassworking. His formula had to be carefully prepared with fine sand, red lead or litharge, potash, and lime. The soda and potash glass continued to be used on the Continent and in early American glasshouses. However, both Stiegel and Amelung made some of the lead glasses. After 1800 and up to 1864 most American tableware was made with lead. In the latter year, William Leighton, Sr. improved the soda-lime formula so well that the making of expensive lead glass was discontinued in most factories. Pressed glass from that time on rarely contained lead which had given the earlier ware weight, brilliance, and resonance. Since 1900 some radically new formulas have been invented, but few have affected table or ornamental ware.

DECORATING METHODS

There are two major methods of decorating glass. First, the decoration is an integral part of the glass. Second, it is added after the article has been otherwise finished. The latter decoration is of two types. Painting, enameling, gilding, and transfer papers give an extrinsic colored decoration. Cutting, engraving, carving, etching, and sandblasting form patterns by removing part of the article.

Decorating glass as it is being formed into articles is accomplished in various ways. With the use of his regular hand tools, a skillful glassblower by blowing, spinning, and reheating can shape an article into different forms. By pinching, pulling out part of it, shaping the rims he can further change its contours. The addition of more glass, either of the same or of a different color, has given glass designers a variety of decorative types. This method includes the simple process of using a few threads around the neck or rim of the article and the complicated technique of imprisoning between two glasses, metals or other glass, either previously patterned or left in flakes or bits.

MOLDS

Making patterns in glass by means of molds is an old and popular method. This is accomplished by either blowing, pressing or pouring the hot metal into the mold. As soon as the blowing iron was invented, glass was blown into clay molds which not only shaped the object but gave it a pattern. In the nineteenth century, clay was still used, but molds made of hard woods, brass, copper, and iron soon displaced clay.

The earliest molds were made in one piece which meant the top of the mold must be its widest part. These "dip" or "open top" molds were also used extensively to impress a gather of glass. Instead of finishing the piece to the size of the mold, it was expanded into a larger article as in pattern-molding. Full-size piece molds, often called "open and shut," are made of two or more parts hinged together. This allows an article of uneven dimensions to be shaped entirely in a mold. At first even these did not finish the piece; rims, handles, collars, feet, and necks had to be done by hand. During the nineteenth

74. *"Open and shut," two-piece iron mold for a "Booze" bottle. Philadelphia Museum of Art.*

century, molds were improved. New ways of molding whole articles were invented. By the latter part of the century even the defects caused in the glass by contact with the metal were somewhat removed by chilling the iron molds. With the introduction of automatic machines, molds and moldmaking were further improved. However, the making of molds has always been a costly part of the process and has required skilled workers.

Molds are filled in three ways. The glass is gathered on the blowing iron and blown into the mold until it contacts the inner surface. This requires skill and practice on the part of the glassblower. If it is a piece mold, an apprentice usually operates the handles. For hand-pressed glass, the hot glass is gathered on a rod, cut off with shears, and allowed to drop into the mold. For machine-blown or pressed ware, the hot glass is automatically poured into the mold.

The most significant contributions that American glassworkers have made to glassmaking is in the field of mass production of automatic machinery for tableware, laboratory, industrial, and architectural glass.

Most collectors of glass are interested in knowing how their treasures were made. The best way to understand the intricate art of fabricating glassware is to see it done. However, few collectors have the opportunity of seeing many types of blown and pressed glass made and decorated. Reading about the processes and then studying each piece will familiarize the collector with the art of glassmaking. It will also help him to choose authentic glass for his collection.

X. COLLECTING ANTIQUE GLASS

Everyone, it seems, has the urge to collect either something modern or antique. A tablesetting of pressed ware of the 1880s or a cabinet of lovely old American glass will please different people. There are diverse opinions about antique collections and there are few definite rules for a new collector to follow.

Many are puzzled by the word antique. In 1931 the United States Treasury Department for purposes of establishing customs duties, declared that any work of art made before 1830 (except rugs, carpets, and musical instruments), should be considered an antique. Thus the object would be at least one hundred years old.

Most lexicographers agree that an antique is an article belonging to a much earlier period than the present. To the people of our young country, fifty years may seem as long as several hundred to Europeans, or several thousands to Egyptians. Everything is relative.

There are reasons, however, for choosing the year 1830. It is considered the beginning of the machine age, the ending of the era of handicrafts. From about that time on Americans emphasized mass production and standardization, rather than quality.

For those who insist that only handmade articles are worth considering, the glass collector can point out that most nineteenth-century glass was made by skilled craftsmen. It was hand-pressed and, during the first half of the century, hand-finished. The so-called art glasses of the late Victorian era were blown and decorated by hand. Intricate molds made by skilled artisans were used by equally skilled glassblowers. In fact glassmaking required almost as much skill in the 1800s as it had in previous centuries.

COLLECT FOR FUN

Fortunately the satisfaction of collecting is not necessarily based on the age of articles nor on workmanship nor on former use. Whether you collect Renaissance Venetian, Anglo-Irish, *Blown Three-mold,* or pressed glass of the 1890s, your enthusiasm and joy of ownership can be the same. That is as it should be, for collecting brings its own satisfaction.

The development of a collection will add to your knowledge of the art of glassworking, the customs of a period, and the history of the times. It will also take you to new places to obtain new pieces for your collection and perhaps best of all, to form new friendships.

Much of the joy of collecting is in the search. Don't be afraid to make mistakes. The best authorities have made them before you. While it may be expensive at the moment, charge it off to acquisition of knowledge. Since learning about your collection is part of the fun, read extensively on the subject, but remember mistakes are also made in print and that new material replaces old. Everyday new information is found to change old "facts" or substantiate new theories.

Unlike some of the other handicrafts, American glass can seldom be identified with one factory or even allocated to one district. Because it is a cooperative craft, scarcely ever has the master craftsman, the glassblower or decorator, signed his name on an article. Some early American articles were marked with the name of the factory. After trade-marks came into use in the late nineteenth century, a great deal of pressed glass was trade-marked on the bottom by cutting into the mold. L. C. Tiffany was one of the first designers to mark his wares. Since he insisted that every piece should be marked with his name or initials, his glass is easier to authenticate.

After you decide what kind of glass or pattern to buy, you will be wise to familiarize yourself with your choice by reading the specialty books. You should also talk to well-informed dealers in antiques. If possible, visit museums that have authenticated examples of your type of glass. Such large institutions as the Metropolitan Museum of Art in New York City, the Museum of Fine Arts in Boston, the Art Institute of Chicago, the Carnegie Museum at Pittsburgh, and the Toledo Museum of Art have excellent collections of glass.

If there is a well-known collector in your town, ask to see his collection. Almost everyone likes to show his treasures and is glad to give suggestions or information.

It is a good idea to have a purpose for your collection. Some people feel it should be kept to the number of items that the owner can easily display. Others point out that many people enjoy arranging a large collection in their homes and showing it to other enthusiasts. However, it is nice to sell duplicates or pieces that are packed away. After all, it gives other people a chance to have the experiences you have been enjoying. All collections should be sorted or weeded out from time to time.

Another useful thing to do with your collection is to loan it to schools, libraries, or for display in store windows. Work out a system for exhibiting your glass. Mark each piece and keep a list with the number and description. (If your collection is insured, this list is required.) It is also wise to put down the price you paid and where you bought the article. Some collectors keep scrapbooks which include magazine clippings about the type they collect, pictures of the collection, newspaper accounts of the exhibits, and even sketches. Sharing your collection with others will often reward you in most unexpected ways. One collector received anonymously a cut glass cruet to add to her collection which she was displaying in a bank window.

Building or decorating a house around a collection is lots of fun and gives a purpose for your glass. A Cincinnati couple had shelves arranged between the dining room and living room to display their beautiful pitchers. Some Cleveland enthusiasts designed their dining room especially to display their large collection of *Amberina* ware.

Some business houses (such as restaurants, banks, inns, and specialty stores) use small or large collections for decorative purposes. A wine cellar at Hammondsport, New York, has a display cabinet with a number of pieces of old glass including a Stiegel-type drug bottle. Rare pieces should be kept in a cabinet (locked or unlocked according to the location). Such pieces should eventually go to a museum.

Many collectors plan to leave their entire collection to a museum. Investigate first as to whether the chosen museum wishes it or needs the kind of glass you have. Perhaps it would be better to send it to another type of museum, or allow it to be sold for other collectors. That is also a way of giving pleasure to many people. Of course, if you have children who are interested in your collection, you will want to consider their wishes. The size of the collection—perhaps part of it should be loaned or given to a museum now—the rarity of the articles, and the need of the museum should be considered.

REPRODUCTIONS

A large number of reproductions, especially in pressed ware, are being manufactured. Those sold with the factory label are usually found in department stores or gift shops. Unfortunately, there are some small glass companies that are making unmarked reproductions. These appear for sale as originals in antique shops with or without the dealer's knowledge. The reproductions made in the early 1930s are harder to spot since they include some blown glass, such as *Burmese* and pictorial bottles. Ruth Webb Lee's revised *Antique Fakes and Reproductions* is helpful for checking up on your pattern. Usually there are some discrepancies between the old and the new glass. If you are paying a large price for a piece, ask for a statement of authenticity from the dealer and the privilege of returning the article within a stated time.

ANTIQUES STUDY CLUBS

For those of you who want company in your search for either an addition to your collection or to your store of knowledge, a membership in an antiques study club or a purely glass study club is well worth while. The former can include your friend who collects china; the latter will undoubtedly give you more immediate knowledge of your chosen field. Both types of clubs can be located through magazines devoted to antiques.

As an Englishman, writing on the collection of old glass said, "Good hunting."

GLOSSARY

Applied handle or decoration. Formed with a separate gather of hot metal which is applied to the body of the article.

Batch. Ingredients of a glass formula ready for melting.

"Black" glass. Dark glass of great color density.

Blanks. Blown or pressed glass articles designed and made for a cut or engraved decoration (also for enameling and staining).

Blowing iron or blowpipe. Hollow iron pipe used to gather and blow glass.

Blown-molded. Glass blown into a mold for pattern or shape or both.

Blown Three-mold. Name given to specific patterns of blown-molded glass made during the early 1800s. This glass was blown in full-size pattern molds usually of three sections.

Bottle glass. Glass made from natural materials, no coloring or decolorizing agents added, usually green but also amber.

Cameo glass. A cased glass with the design sculptured in low relief on the outer layer (or layers) of glass.

Cased. Glass containing two or more layers, usually of contrasting colors. See plating.

Crystal. Very clear colorless glass; transparent quartz.

119

Dip mold. Open-top one-piece mold.

Fire-polishing. Removing mold marks or other defects by reheating.

Flint. The term for crystal glass. First used in England when crystal was made of pulverized flint. This was later replaced by ordinary silica with lead.

Free-blown. Hand-blown, made with glassblower's tools, but without molds.

Full-size piece mold. A mold made of two or more parts the same size as the finished article.

Gadroon. Flutes or ribbing on an added layer of glass that is pulled part way over an article.

Gather. Molten metal (glass) taken from the furnace on the end of blowing iron.

Glory hole. Small furnace used for reheating articles and fire-polishing.

Heat-sensitive opal glass. A kind of glass which becomes opaque in proportion to the degree of heat.

Lacy. Pressed glass with a finely stippled background.

Lampworker. Term used to designate a glassblower who forms articles from rods and tubes of glass by working them over a blast lamp.

Latticinio. An opaque white cane of glass flattened into a network of squares or a ribbon of filigree and cased in clear glass.

Lead glass. Glass containing lead oxide usually in relatively large amounts.

Lily-pad. Name given to a free-blown glass which was decorated with superimposed glass worked into the form of a lily pad (late eighteenth and early nineteenth centuries).

Metal. Molten or cold glass.

Millefiori. Italian for "a thousand flowers." The term is used for cased glass which has a mosaic of glass canes with various colored patterns (previously made in molds), enclosed in clear glass.

Molded. Usually refers to glass blown into a mold to give shape, pattern, or both.

Offhand. Glass made outside the general run (usually from tag end of batch), by workers for their own use or pleasure.

Ohio-Stiegel. Blown glass made in Pennsylvania, West Virginia, and Ohio in the Stiegel traditions (or techniques), usually pattern-molded.

Overlay. This term is popularly applied to a Victorian cased ware in which the outside layer (or layers) was partially cut away to form a pattern. It is also used to describe a glass of more than one layer. See plating.

Pattern-molded. Glass blown into part-size mold (dip or piece molds), to give it a pattern; article is then expanded to full size and finished.

Pillar-molded. Term applied to a blown-molded glass of more than one gather of metal which produced a heavy ware with vertical ribs or "pillars" outside and left the inside of the article smooth (patternless).

Plating, lining, flashing, casing. Putting together two or three layers of glass by one of several methods.

Pontil mark. Scar on bottom of article left when it is cracked off of pontil (puntee or punty) rod which is used to hold glass while it is being finished.

Pressed glass. Articles made by pressing hot metal into molds.

Prunt. A small blob of glass applied to article, left plain or designed; example, leaf prunt.

Quilling. Ribbons of applied glass that are pinched into waves: pincered trailing.

Soda-lime glass. Made from a silica, soda, lime formula. In 1864 Leighton's new formula contained bicarbonate of soda which replaced poor grades of soda ash and made a clearer, more brilliant glass.

Stiegel-type. Glass made and decorated in techniques apparently used at Stiegel's glasshouses in Pennsylvania.

Stippling. In pressed glass, a background of small raised dots close together.

Superimposed decoration. Glass added to the body of the piece and tooled in some manner, such as, lily pad and gadrooning.

Threading. Fine threads of hot glass added as decoration; also done by machine in the late nineteenth century.

Whimseys. Term used by glass collectors to cover odd or unusual pieces and glass toys.

"Witch" balls. A whimsey (reportedly used in England to keep away witches), which displayed the glassblower's skill.

ABOUT THE AUTHOR

Valentine Van Tassel's interest in the art of glassmaking commenced when she moved to Corning, New York, in 1930. The various types of art glass made there fascinated her, as did the history of industrial glass exemplified by the work of the Corning Glass Works. She began to study and to collect glass. Her research included visits to the sites of early American glasshouses in Virginia, Pennsylvania, and Massachusetts, and the study of glass fragments taken from these locations. She has watched the production of many kinds of glass from plate glass made on completely automatic machines to glass pharmaceutical ware, glass eyes and glass miniatures, handmade by skilled lampworkers. She has contacted personally and by letter hundreds of people who either work with glass or own glass collections. Her own unusual collection illustrates the art of glassmaking from early times to the latest domestic and industrial glassware.

Eventually this hobby led her into lecturing to women's clubs, men's groups, antiques clubs, college classes, museums, and even department stores. Writing about glass was the next step. Valentine Van Tassel is a regular contributor of articles on American glass to the *Antiques Jour-*

nal. She also conducts a question-and-answer column in that magazine.

On travels in England, on the Continent, and to the Near East, she has visited various kinds of glass factories ranging all the way from large modern plants to a one-room adobe glasshouse in Palestine. Her interest in glass led to the study of the art of stained glass. She studied this in the great cathedrals abroad, in churches in the United States, and also in the outstanding stained-glass studios in America.

The author is a graduate of the University of Wisconsin where she met her husband, Edwin M. Guyer, while he was studying for a doctorate in physics. Dr. Guyer is associated with the research laboratory of the Corning Glass Works.

INDEX

126